THE OFFICIAL
ENGLAND
EURO 2004 GUIDE

ENGLAND

Steve Bidmead

CONTENTS

CARLTON
BOOKS

England's route to the Finals

England's group came down to the final match, but then again you wouldn't want things to get boring, would you? There may have been a couple of low points during England's Euro 2004 qualifying campaign, but Eriksson's men made it. Here's a match-by-match reminder of just how the Lions roared...

Match 1
Slovakia 1–2 England
12 OCTOBER 2002, BRATISLAVA

England, favourites to win the group, started their first qualifying match slowly. They couldn't settle down and struggled to come to terms with the wet conditions in Slovakia.

The hosts, on the other hand, were switched on right from the kick-off, resulting in a goal from Middlesbrough striker Szilard Nemeth in the 24th minute.

England dominated the second half, though, and captain David Beckham scored with a trademark free-kick from the left, with Michael Owen a breath away from getting the final touch. In the 82nd minute, Owen headed home the winner from a Paul Scholes (pictured above) cross. Owen's headed goals became a regular sight in the group.

England line up
Seaman
G Neville
Cole
Gerrard (Dyer 77)
Woodgate
Southgate
Beckham
Scholes
Heskey (Smith 90)
Owen (Hargreaves 85)
Butt

Match 2
England 2–2 FYR Macedonia
16 OCTOBER 2002, SOUTHAMPTON

It was a tough game for England. Taking the lead twice during the game, it was the Macedonian players who left the pitch as heroes. After just ten minutes, Artim Sakiri's corner kick looped over David Seaman's head and straight into the net!

England line up
Seaman
G Neville
Cole
Gerrard (Butt 55)
Woodgate
Campbell
Beckham
Scholes
Smith
Owen
Bridge (Vassell 58)

England didn't panic, though, and Beckham chipped the keeper to equalize three minutes later. A mistake from Sol Campbell resulted in a 20-metre drive from Vanco Trojanov that made the score 2–1 after 25 minutes, before Steven Gerrard (right) hit England's second from the same distance 35 minutes in.

England had more chances during the rest of the game and, in the final minute, Alan Smith had a close range shot saved before being sent off for a second bookable offence. Nobody was happy.

Match 3

Liechtenstein 0–2 England

29 MARCH 2003, VADUZ

An edgy start from England, who desperately needed to put the memory of Macedonia behind them.

Liechtenstein managed a couple of shots to test new regular keeper David James but then England's first classy move resulted in a goal. Liverpool's Emile Heskey crossed to club-mate Owen, who (again) headed into the back of the net to claim his 20th England goal in his 46th match.

Confidence up, England dominated the game and just eight minutes into the second half, Beckham lashed in a 20-metre free-kick (his tenth goal for his country) to secure all three points. England were back.

England line up
James
G Neville
Bridge
Gerrard (Butt 66)
Ferdinand
Southgate
Beckham (Murphy 70)
Scholes
Heskey (Rooney 80)
Owen
Dyer

Match 4

England 2–0 Turkey

2 APRIL 2003, SUNDERLAND

This was Everton sensation Wayne Rooney's first competitive start and he was the star of the show, inspiring England to their best performance in the group so far.

Both sides were really determined, and Beckham was booked in the ninth minute. Three minutes later he shot just wide. Turkey had never scored against England and with Ferdinand and Campbell strong at the back, that seemed unlikely to change.

Owen went off injured in the second half and his replacement Darius Vassell scored the opening goal after 75 minutes. Scholes and Ferdinand had chances from a corner before the ball reached the Aston Villa star, who fired from close range. In injury time, Kieron Dyer was fouled in the box and ultra-reliable Beckham slotted home the penalty kick.

England line up
James
G Neville
Bridge
Gerrard
Ferdinand
Campbell
Beckham
Scholes
Rooney (Dyer 88)
Owen (Vassell 57)
Butt

Match 5
England 2–1 Slovakia
11 JUNE 2003, MIDDLESBROUGH

Against Slovakia, Owen became the youngest player to win 50 England caps and with Beckham suspended, he was also made captain for the day.

As early as the first minute, Owen looked sharp, shooting just wide. But, as they had in the first meeting, it was Slovakia who scored first, this time from a Vladimir Janocko free-kick. The visitors had a number of chances to go even further ahead.

In the 62nd minute Owen saved the day – he took on the whole of the Slovakia defence and won a penalty, which he duly scored. Southgate had a penalty appeal turned down, and Lampard had a goal disallowed for offside before Owen scored yet another header from a pinpoint Gerrard cross. He couldn't manage the hat-trick but it was Owen's day.

England line up
James
Mills (Hargreaves 43)
Cole
Gerrard
Upson
Southgate
Lampard
Scholes
Rooney (Vassell 58)
Owen
P Neville

Match 6
FYR Macedonia 1–2 England
6 SEPTEMBER 2003, SKOPJE

Wayne Rooney became England's youngest goalscorer ever, aged 17 and 317 days, as England set a post-war record of seven successive wins.

Former Barnsley striker Georgi Hristov opened the scoring in the 28th minute, mid-way through a frustrating first half for toothless England. Artim Sakiri, scorer in the first game and newly-signed for West Bromwich Albion, was the game's most impressive player.

Beckham was fit to play after picking up an injury at new club Real Madrid, but both Paul Scholes and Steven Gerrard were out, replaced by Frank Lampard and Owen Hargreaves.

When Emile Heskey came on for Lampard, he quickly set up Rooney, who shot first time from the edge of the box to equalize. When John Terry was tripped in the box on 63 minutes, David Beckham scored another penalty to save English blushes.

England line up
James
G Neville
Cole
Hargreaves
Terry
Campbell
Beckham
Lampard (Heskey 46)
Rooney (P Neville 74)
Owen (Dyer 84)
Butt

Match 7
England 2–0 Liechtenstein
10 SEPTEMBER 2003, MANCHESTER

Returning to Old Trafford for the first time since quitting Manchester United for Real Madrid, Beckham helped England extend their record-winning run.

Liechtenstein's hard work in defence kept the home side at bay for the first half, although Beckham and James Beattie both hit the crossbar. Again, England needed two second half goals to secure maximum points, which meant they would only need a draw against their group rivals Turkey.

Steven Gerrard was instrumental in both, crossing for Owen to score another header, then setting up Rooney for his 52nd minute goal. Liechtenstein's only shot on goal came in the last minute but James saved it well.

England line up
James
G Neville
Bridge
Gerrard (P Neville 57)
Terry
Upson
Beckham (Hargreaves 57)
Lampard
Rooney (J Cole 67)
Owen
Beattie

Match 8
Turkey 0–0 England
11 OCTOBER 2003, ISTANBUL

The all-important decider. Which team would finish top of the group and qualify automatically? England started better than Turkey without creating any clear chances. After 36 minutes Gerrard was tripped by Tugay in the box and England were awarded a penalty. But amazingly captain Beckham slipped as he struck it and the ball ballooned over. The tension mounted.

By the second half, England were being forced backwards, especially by Turkey's danger man Nihat. Later, Beckham headed into the net, but Dyer, who'd supplied the ball, was judged to be offside.

Afterwards, Turkey boss Senol Gunes congratulated England on qualification, and given the difficult circumstances before and during the match, it was a great result.
Next stop: Euro 2004!

England line up
James
G Neville
Cole
Gerrard
Terry
Campbell
Beckham
Scholes (Lampard 90)
Rooney (Dyer 72)
Heskey (Vassell 76)
Butt

Group 7 Final Table	P	W	D	L	F	A	Pts
England	8	6	2	0	14	5	20
Turkey	8	6	1	1	17	5	19
Slovakia	8	3	1	4	11	9	10
Macedonia	8	1	3	4	11	14	6
Liechtenstein	8	0	1	7	2	22	1

Profile:
Sven-Goran Eriksson

Sven-Goran Eriksson has spent so long on England's motorways that he could probably drive from London to Manchester with his eyes closed! From the moment he quit Italian club Lazio to take the England job he has attended countless Premiership matches – as many as 20 a month. Sometimes it's like he's in two places at once!

Despite the constant media attention, Eriksson has turned the nation's fortunes around, taking England to the Japan/South Korea 2002 World Cup. And now he has guided Beckham, Owen, Rooney and the other stars to Portugal, where they hope to lift the trophy.

In 2001, Eriksson enjoyed the best start of any England manager ever – five

Eriksson's first match as England manager:

VILLA PARK, 28 FEBRUARY 2001
England 3–0 Spain
Barmby, Heskey
Ehiogu

England line up
James (Martyn 46)
P Neville (G Neville 78)
Powell (Ball 46)
Butt (Lampard 46)
Ferdinand (Ehiogu 46)
Campbell
Beckham (Heskey 46)
Scholes (McCann 46)
A Cole
Owen
Barmby

Eriksson and his captain discuss tactics.

Sven the Manager	
1976	Manager, Degerfors (Sweden)
1979	Manager, IFK Gothenburg (Sweden) – won league title, Swedish Cup (twice) and UEFA Cup
1982	Manager, Benfica (Portugal) – won league title (twice) and Portuguese Cup
1984	Manager, Roma (Italy) – won Italian Cup
1987	Manager, Fiorentina (Italy)
1989	Manager, Benfica (Portugal) – won league title
1992	Manager, Sampdoria (Italy) – won Italian Cup
1997	Manager, Lazio (Italy) – won UEFA Cup-Winners Cup, UEFA Super Cup, league title, Italian Cup and Italian Super Cup

straight wins. Then, his side's amazing 5–1 win over Germany in Munich created a huge feelgood factor and his popularity went through the roof. Fans thought it must be a dream.

Two years later, those same fans thought the 3–1 friendly defeat at home to Australia in February 2003 must be a terrible nightmare. Coming after a disappointing Euro 2004 qualifying draw with minnows FYR Macedonia, the England manager suddenly found himself under intense pressure.

The 0–0 draw in Istanbul against Turkey booked England's Euro 2004 ticket and restored faith in the Swedish coach. The build-up to the game had been more intense than any in recent memory, but Eriksson – always the calmest man in the stadium – was not distracted from his task.

Sven's serious.

Sven the Player

Born on 5 February 1948 in Torsby, Sweden – a town of 4,000 where they still call him 'Svennis' – Eriksson became a hard-working right-back. He played for his local club and then for Degerfors and Karlskoga, before injury forced his retirement, aged just 27.

It is almost four years since he said 'Yes' to the offer of the England job. At the time, the entire population was split over the issue of appointing a foreign coach, but now those arguments are long-forgotten and Sven has become a part of everyday life in England.

He is an intelligent man who speaks four languages and reads Tibetan poetry, is introverted and hides his emotions, but he skilfully wins the respect of his players by keeping things simple. The ice-cool mastermind is familiar with Portugal – he managed top team Benfica twice. Now he returns to the sunshine to face the biggest challenge of his career as England go for glory at Euro 2004.

Did you know?

Under Eriksson, England have lost just one competitive match – the 2–1 defeat by Brazil in the World Cup quarter-final.

Michael Owen

Position | Striker **Date of Birth** | 14.12.1979 **Club** | Liverpool

The 2001 European Footballer of the Year is a striker of pure class who enjoys the big stage. His three goals against Germany in the famous 5–1 win made him a legend and he has also won the FA Cup, the UEFA Cup, the League Cup and the UEFA Super Cup with his club.

But perhaps because Liverpool haven't won the Premiership title, people sometimes forget just how awesome Owen is.

His career began with a bang when he scored on his Liverpool debut against Wimbledon in 1997. The following season he became the youngest player to: 1) be top scorer in the English top flight (18 goals); 2) play for England (vs Chile in February 1998); 3) score for England (vs Morocco in May 1998); and 4) score for England at a World Cup (vs Romania).

Though serious injury has sometimes threatened his electric pace, Owen has always bounced back and proved himself a single-minded goal machine, deadly with either foot as well as his head (despite being just 5ft 9in).

Now 24 years old, Euro 2004 should be the tournament when the world sees the very best of Michael Owen, a superstar at the peak of his career. If he can repeat the amazing goal against Argentina at the 1998 World Cup, when he skipped through the entire opposition defence and blasted the ball into the back of the net, then England can beat anyone.

Wayne Rooney

Position | Striker   **Date of Birth** | 24.10.1985   **Club** | Everton

Rooney is unique. There is not another player in the world like him. He became England's youngest ever international when he made his debut in the ill-fated friendly against Australia last February.

In that game he showed no signs of nerves and the tide of 'Rooneymania' that has swept the nation is in no danger of dying down.

'Roonaldo' is the most exciting English player since Paul Gascoigne, but while Gazza's talents were wasted, Rooney has been carefully protected by David Moyes, his manager at Everton.

Despite that, Sven-Goran Eriksson decided Rooney was ready to play regularly for his country and the young striker is now as famous as Beckham and Owen. His fiery temper has landed him in trouble a few times while his bull-like physique and brilliant skill give even the best defenders sleepless nights.

Rooney was always destined for greatness. In one season as a ten-year-old, he scored 99 goals. His family home in Liverpool was adorned with Everton flags and scarves, and he visited Goodison Park when six months old, so there was no doubt which club he would eventually play for. But few people could have predicted the impact he would make for club and country at such a young age.

Many experts claim he has the best 'football brain' in the game, others insist he is a genius, as good as the legendary George Best.

Rooney has moved out of that old family house now, and is earning a fortune from football. But he is still the same lad who loved a kickabout on the streets of Croxteth.

David Beckham

Position | Midfielder   Date of Birth | 02.05.1975   Club | Real Madrid

One of the most famous faces on the planet, Beckham lives his life under the constant attention of the world's media.

But he is much more than just a pretty face, a haircut and a curling free-kick. Above all, he is a great all-round midfielder and England's inspirational captain. His performance against Greece – which single-handedly took England to the 2002 World Cup – will be remembered as one of the most courageous of any player in an England shirt. Ever. And in many of the Euro 2004 qualifying games he was just as impressive, as he ran tirelessly for 90 minutes.

Some people doubted that he would be good enough to succeed amongst the star-studded cast that is Real Madrid after last summer's transfer from Manchester United, the club he signed for as a schoolboy. But he has proved the critics wrong and is a regular in the team that boasts international superstars like Figo, Zidane and Ronaldo.

Beckham is often admired for the way he puts family values above all else, and screamed at by teenage girls wherever he goes, Beckham is the ultimate advert for football. Occasionally his temper boils over, as it did against Turkey last autumn, and opponents regularly try to get him booked, but his cultured right foot does the talking. There is no-one better at striking a dead ball, and his ratio of goals from free-kicks is amazing.

Ever since that 60-yard lob over Wimbledon keeper Neil Sullivan in 1996, the Beckham phenomenon has grown. His ideas, pin-point passing and leadership qualities will be the most vital part of England's bid to win the 2004 European Championship.

Steven Gerrard

| Position | Midfielder | Date of Birth | 30.05.1980 | Club | Liverpool |

A lot of players have been labelled 'the future of England' in the last decade, but Steven George Gerrard is the real deal. Tall, strong, aggressive and intelligent, the Liverpool man is key to England's style of play.

Whether he is used as a holding midfielder just in front of the defenders, further forward in support of the strikers, or even on the wing, Gerrard's presence gives the team a boost.

Gerrard came up through the youth ranks at Liverpool with Michael Owen, and his first trip to Wembley was with Owen when the youngsters watched Liverpool play Leeds. But while the striker's career took off way back in 1997, the midfielder nicknamed 'Stevie G' had to wait a bit longer for his chance. His club debut came during the 1998–99 season against Spanish club Celta Vigo, and he became a first choice the following season. He endured fitness problems as he rapidly grew to 6ft 1in tall, but now that he has stopped getting taller (probably!) he can focus on his growing reputation.

Gerrard is often compared to Roy Keane and Patrick Vieira and he is truly in their class – one of the world's best.

His limitless energy, Beckham-like passing and will to win are important ingredients in the England recipe. Since his debut against Ukraine in May 2000, Gerrard has proved he can hold the England midfield together, and fans are looking forward to evem more great perform-ances in Portugal.

Sol Campbell

Position | Defender   Date of Birth | 18.09.1974   Club | Arsenal

This intimidating centre-back is one of England's senior players and one of the world's finest defenders. Powerful in the air and on the ground, experienced and calm, he has been a reliable figure at the back for his country for almost ten years.

He made his international debut as a 21-year-old sub in the 3–0 win over Hungary in May 1996 and went on to play at the Euro 96 tournament, held in England. He then became England's youngest captain since Bobby Moore in a game against Belgium in May 1998. One of the nation's best performers at the 1998 World Cup, Euro 2000 and the 2002 World Cup, Campbell became hot property.

He angered fans of Tottenham Hotspur – the club he'd played for since his scoring debut in 1992 – when he joined arch-rivals Arsenal in 2001. The move was even more shocking considering Barcelona, Inter Milan and Bayern Munich were interested too.

The decision to quit Spurs was a very hard one to make but he has become a better, more experienced player at Arsenal, league and cup winners in 2002. Arsenal manager Arsene Wenger calls Campbell his 'super rock'.

Recent years have seen the rise of excellent defenders such as John Terry, Jonathan Woodgate and Rio Ferdinand as rivals for a place in the England side. But Campbell's lightning pace and confidence mean he is the nation's most dependable barrier at the back, as well as being dangerous at set pieces. His acting debut in the ITV drama *Footballers' Wives* could signal a new career when he finally stops playing. This quiet, thoughtful footballer could probably turn his hand to anything.

David James

Position | Goalkeeper   Date of Birth | 01.08.1970   Club | Manchester City

David James used to be known as 'The Vampire' because he didn't like crosses! But the brilliant shot-stopper, who began his career at Watford before spells with Liverpool, Aston Villa, West Ham and his current club Manchester City, has become England's first-choice 'keeper.

The towering star spent much of this season in the English First Division following West Ham's relegation from the Premiership, but Sven-Goran Eriksson kept faith with him and his return to the Premiership has been a boost for the coach, the team and the player.

James made his England debut in 1997 against Mexico but for years faced a battle with Nigel Martyn to be David Seaman's understudy on the international scene. Still just 33 – relatively young for a goalkeeper – he has time to add to his 20-odd caps while England wait for youngsters Chris Kirkland and Paul Robinson to mature. David's patient wait for the end of the Seaman era of England goalkeeping has finally paid off – and he even took over from the pony-tailed ex-Arsenal player between the sticks at Manchester City!

Bleached-blond bombshell James also has an interesting life away from football. He enjoys painting and has even modelled on the catwalk! The good-looking goalie with the artistic side is more substance than style, though. Since quitting Villa for West Ham in 2001 and then Manchester City in 2004, his performances have convinced not only Eriksson of his suitability for the England jersey but 99 per cent of England supporters as well. David James has earned his place.

Paul Scholes

Position | Midfielder   **Date of Birth** | 16.11.1974   **Club** | Manchester United

As a youngster, Salford-born Scholes was the most promising of 'Fergie's Fledglings' – the group of young players Sir Alex Ferguson nurtured that also included Beckham, Giggs, Butt and the Nevilles. Scholes has fulfilled his potential, becoming one of the most effective attacking midfielders in world football. Prolific for his club, particularly when deployed behind the main strikers, he could rediscover his scoring touch for England at this tournament.

He first played for Glenn Hoddle's England in 1997, in a friendly against South Africa at Old Trafford. Scholes was also a key figure in United's glorious 1999 Champions League campaign, though he was suspended for the final. A fiery, energetic player, he will be looking for even more silverware this summer.

Rio Ferdinand

Position | Defender   **Date of Birth** | 07.11.1978   **Club** | Manchester United

England's best player at the 2002 World Cup, Ferdinand became the world's most expensive defender for the second time on his return from the tournament in the Far East. Manchester United offered Leeds United £30 million for the stylish centre-back and the Yorkshire club couldn't say no. Two years before that, Leeds had made West Ham United a world record £18 million offer they couldn't refuse.

From the moment Ferdinand led West Ham to the 1996 FA Youth Cup final, he was labelled the new Bobby Moore. His calm assurance on the ball, his ability to play his way out of trouble, combined with strength and power convinced observers he would go on to become one of England's greats.

Wayne Bridge

Position | Defender   **Date of Birth** | 05.08.1980   **Club** | Chelsea

An exciting young left-back, Bridge is famous for rarely getting injured, and was the only outfield player from any team to play in every single game of the 2000–01 Premiership season, and he was named Southampton's player of the year in the process.

In 2003 Bridge became part of Chelsea's 'Russian Revolution' last July in a £7 million transfer from Southampton, where he'd been playing since 1997.

Facing a battle with Arsenal's Ashley Cole for the left-back slot in the national side – a battle that could result in Eriksson playing both of them – he is a player capable of matching the very best in the world. The 23-year-old is solid in defence and clever in attack. Bridge's cultured left foot could be an effective weapon in Portugal.

Emile Heskey

Position | Striker   **Date of Birth** | 11.01.1978   **Club** | Liverpool

Heskey is a muscular, big-hitting figure and the focal point of many England attacks. Although he can hold off opponents with his strength and get his head onto long balls, Heskey's main strength is in fact on the ground. With quick feet – which occasionally get themselves in a tangle! – and the ability to run at defenders, he is one of the Premiership's toughest, most explosive forwards.

Never as prolific as Liverpool team-mate Michael Owen (though he has scored over 50 goals for his current club), his movement and physical attributes open gaps for other England players to get into scoring positions.

Frank Lampard

Position | Midfielder   **Date of Birth** | 21.06.1978   **Club** | Chelsea

Frank Lampard's father – also called Frank – won the FA Cup twice with West Ham United. But when Frank Senior left his job as Assistant Manager at the club and the Hammers then sold Rio Ferdinand to Leeds, Frank Junior decided to move on too. Chelsea was the destination and he has become an automatic choice in their dazzling all-star line-up. The former England Under-21 star has improved a lot in the last two seasons, and he is now a player of immense football intelligence and quality. Like Steven Gerrard, he can play a holding role or join the forwards near the opposition penalty box. 'Lamps' is a top class midfielder who would strengthen any side he plays in and is looking forward to his first international tournament.

Gary Neville

Position | Defender   **Date of Birth** | 18.02.1975   **Club** | Manchester United

Few players have played anywhere near as many Champions League games as Gary Neville. Since making his senior Manchester United debut in a game against Torpedo Moscow in 1992, the older of the two Neville brothers has become an almost permanent sight in Europe's biggest club competition.

Transferring his success at youth level into the senior side, Neville has made the right-back position his own for club and country – despite competition from his brother Phil – and has a great understanding with David Beckham on that side of the pitch. His combination of tireless running, solid tackling and impressive attacking know-how make him one of the world's most successful defenders.

John Terry

Position | Defender   **Date of Birth** | 07.12.1980   **Club** | Chelsea

Terry's England debut came in June 2003 in a friendly against Serbia and Montenegro, a game that represented a comeback in the young centre-back's career, for he had not even been considered for the 2002 World Cup squad. The former England Under-21 captain needed to re-evaluate himself and has come back stronger than ever. Playing Champions League football alongside French internationals Marcel Desailly and William Gallas at Chelsea has helped improve his game and he is now one of the best defenders in the country. Strong and determined, he is dominant in the air and more skilful than many give him credit for.

James Beattie

Position | Striker   **Date of Birth** | 27.02.1978   **Club** | Southampton

People used to think Beattie was only a form player whose goals came in short spurts followed by long droughts, but he has been consistently excellent for the last two years. The England manager needs a strong centre forward in case Heskey is injured and although Beattie is not as aggressive as, say, Alan Shearer, his power and movement in the box give defenders a headache. Injury and poor form damaged his early career, but the 2002–03 season saw him find his feet, as well as bag 24 goals. The England call-up did not come until the February 2003 game against Australia, and although Owen and Rooney grab most of the headlines, Beattie has done enough to be considered international class.

Ashley Cole

Position | Defender   **Date of Birth** | 20.12.1980   **Club** | Arsenal

Ashley Cole started out as a striker at Highbury's Centre of Excellence before making his first team debut against Middlesbrough in the 1999 League Cup. Now a regular at left-back for club and country, he is known for his energy and inventiveness and the attacking skills he developed as a youngster hold him in good stead. His defending – which some people call his one weakness – has improved in recent seasons and he is now calm and confident under pressure. Eriksson included Cole in his very first England squad in February 2001 and the youngster has kept his place, playing in every game at the 2002 World Cup before England went out to Brazil in the quarter-final. Since taking over from Brazilian Silvinho in the Arsenal defence, he has won Premiership, FA Cup and FA Community Shield winner's medals with the club and will surely go on to win even more.

Darius Vassell

Position | Striker   **Date of Birth** | 13.06.1980   **Club** | Aston Villa

In the 1996–97 season, while in the Villa youth team, Vassell broke the club record by scoring 39 goals. He made his senior debut from the bench in August 1998, and the tricky young forward became a hero when he scored the equalizer and winner against Norwegians Stromsgodset in the UEFA Cup. After establishing himself in the Villa starting line-up, he won his first senior England call-up in February 2002 in a friendly against Holland. His spectacular overhead equalizer was the first of three goals in his first six internationals and he endeared himself to the England manager and supporters. The arrival of Wayne Rooney has put the brakes on his amazing rise to the top for a while, but great things are expected of this brilliant striker.

Nicky Butt

Position | Midfielder   Date of Birth | 21.01.1975   Club | Manchester United

Pele, the greatest player of all time, singled out Butt as the best player of the 2002 World Cup. The Manchester United player does not always get the credit he deserves, however. A powerful and intelligent holding midfielder, he has been overshadowed at club level, first by Paul Ince, then Roy Keane. But when he plays, he plays well. For years, other clubs tried to prise him away from Old Trafford but they underestimated his loyalty to his local club. Butt is another of 'Fergie's Fledglings' – the group homegrown of stars who emerged during the 1990s – and he is one of the club's most consistent players. Few players in the England squad have a medal collection to compare with Butt's.

Kieron Dyer

Position | Midfielder   Date of Birth | 29.12.1978   Club | Newcastle United

Usually used as a sub by Eriksson, the elusive Dyer is a great impact player who can run at opponents with pace and creativity. He is something of a mystery, however, and no-one has worked out his best position yet. Able to play on both wings or in central areas, if Dyer hits his top form, he can be England's trump card at the tournament.

Though injury and off-field incidents have hampered his career since he joined Newcastle and made his international debut, he is one of Eriksson's favourite players. As quick as Owen, as skilful as Rooney and as hard-working as Beckham, will Euro 2004 be the stage to finally see the best of Kieron Dyer?

ENGLAND

Setting the scene:
Portugal 2004

On Sunday 4 July 2004, one country's football team will be crowned the best in Europe. Current title holders France begin Euro 2004 as the favourites to reach and win the final in Lisbon, but there are 15 other sides who will do all they can to stop them.

As hosts, Portugal have qualified automatically, and although they don't have the strength in depth of France, Italy, Germany or England, the passion of their home supporters will drive them on. The Euro 2004 logo is designed with Portuguese fans in mind – it is a football within a shining golden heart. The seven green dots on it, incidentally, represent both Portugal's conquests of the seven seas and the seven castles on their national flag.

Portugal is one of Europe's poorest countries, but its economy is on the up and its friendly people absolutely adore their football. Euro 2004 will be the biggest sporting event ever to be held in the country that borders both the Atlantic Ocean and the Mediterranean Sea, and it will be a spectacular festival of talent and colour.

The European Championship is the third most popular sporting event on the planet, behind the World Cup and the Olympics. Like the World Cup, it comes round just once every four years, and when it was held in Belgium and Holland in 2000, the total TV viewing figure for the tournament was over seven billion! One million fans

The sea-faring Portuguese will be on dry land this summer.

The Algarve is a popular destination for British holidaymakers.

attended matches live, and organizers expect similar numbers this summer, as the world's attention shifts to the sunshine of Portugal.

Over the past two years, 200 qualifying games have been played, plus 10 play-off fixtures last November, and now there are just 31 matches left before one nation is crowned king of the continent. 16 of Europe's 52 countries are represented at the tournament, all with different styles of play and varying hopes of success.

England's best performances in the European Championship were reaching the semi-final in 1968 and again in 1996. Historically, Germany is the strongest nation in this competition, reaching five finals and winning three times, while the old Soviet Union reached four finals. The last two finals have been decided by extra-time golden goal winners – from Oliver Bierhoff for Germany in 1996 and then David Trezeguet for France in 2000.

The Euro 2004 mascot, by the way, is Kinas, an energetic sort of lad who was born in a remote Portuguese village, apparently with a supernatural gift. All the skill and knowledge of the world's great footballers, past and present, was somehow passed to him. Thankfully for the 15 other teams in the competition, Kinas will not be in Portugal's starting line-up!

Year	Venue	Final
1960	France	Soviet Union 2–1 Yugoslavia (AET)
1964	Spain	Spain 2–1 Soviet Union
1968	Italy	Italy 1–1 Yugoslavia (AET)
		REPLAY: Italy 2–0 Yugoslavia
1972	Belgium	West Germany 3–0 Soviet Union
1976	Yugoslavia	Czechoslovakia 2–2 West Germany (AET, 5–3 on pens)
1980	Italy	West Germany 2–1 Belgium
1984	France	France 2–0 Spain
1988	West Germany	Holland 2–0 Soviet Union
1992	Sweden	Denmark 2–0 Germany
1996	England	Germany 2–1 Czech Republic (AET)
2000	Bel/Hol	France 2–1 Italy (AET)

The Venues

Euro 2004 is the first time that Portugal has hosted a major football tournament. One of the smallest countries in Europe, it takes less than two hours to make your way from the farthest south venue, Faro, to the farthest north, Braga.

The compact size of the country really favours the staging of Euro 2004, where teams have to move up and down the country as they progress through the tournament. The England team will play its three group matches in two venues: Luz in Lisbon (not Sunderland!) and the Coimbra Municipal in Coimbra. If they get through to the next round they'll be going farther afield and getting to see more of the beautiful countryside.

All of the teams are hoping that they will be making their way to Lisbon at the beginning of July – to Benfica's recently built stadium, the Estadio da Luz – where the final will take place.

The Algarve has more than just great beaches. This is the Estoi Palace in Faro.

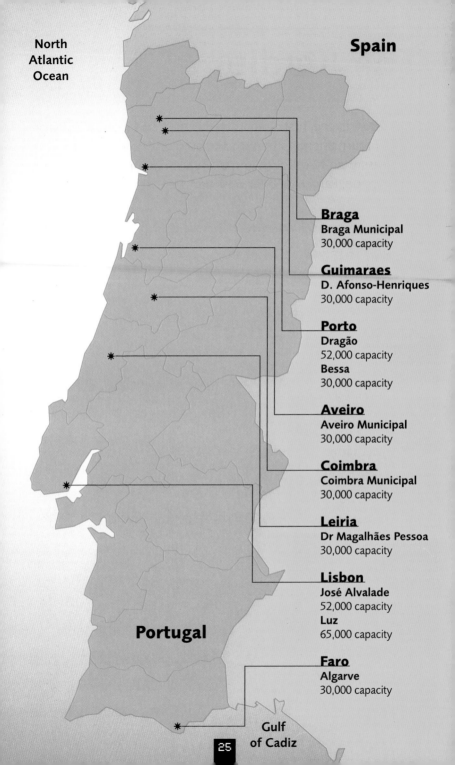

North
Atlantic
Ocean

Spain

Braga
Braga Municipal
30,000 capacity

Guimaraes
D. Afonso-Henriques
30,000 capacity

Porto
Dragão
52,000 capacity
Bessa
30,000 capacity

Aveiro
Aveiro Municipal
30,000 capacity

Coimbra
Coimbra Municipal
30,000 capacity

Leiria
Dr Magalhães Pessoa
30,000 capacity

Lisbon
José Alvalade
52,000 capacity
Luz
65,000 capacity

Faro
Algarve
30,000 capacity

Portugal

Gulf
of Cadiz

The Stadiums

European football's governing body UEFA has praised Portugal for preparing ten magnificent stadiums in three years, calling the achievement a 'miracle'. Seven of the venues are brand new and the other three have been significantly modernized, all at a cost of £550 million.

DRAGÃO (PORTO)
The venue for Euro 2004's opening ceremony and match, the stunning 52,000-seater 'Dragon' Stadium has replaced the old Antas Stadium as the home of Portugal's top club, FC Porto. The see-through roof has been dubbed 'The Veil' and required 280 tonnes of metal to build. Even the surrounding area has been totally transformed in preparation for the tournament.

BESSA (PORTO)
Four new stands have been constructed at the home of Boavista in the city of Porto, making the Bessa Stadium feel like an old-fashioned English ground. The city is best known for its wine (port), bridges and cathedral and this stadium, also incorporating training facilities and tennis courts, is close to all the best sights.

BRAGA MUNICIPAL (BRAGA)
Described as a 'work of art' by UEFA, this elegant new 30,000 all-seater is located in the Monte Castro hillside overlooking the Cávado River. Braga is one of Portugal's oldest and historically most religious cities and is the setting for the tournament's most northerly venue.

AVEIRO MUNICIPAL (AVEIRO)
This ambitious newly-built stadium holds 30,000 spectators and its remarkable design – a bold mix of colour and creativity – make it stand out at this tournament. The surrounding 'Sports Park' also includes six hotels and a golf course. Aveiro is known as 'The Venice of Portugal' because of its canals.

COIMBRA MUNICIPAL (COIMBRA)

Another 30,000-capacity venue, this is a remodelled version of the existing 15,000-capacity stadium. While some of Euro 2004's venues have made historical references in their design, Coimbra has chosen a modern look, using lots of glass. Outside the ground there is a cinema and swimming pool, and there's also an underground car park. Coimbra is known as 'The Oxford of Portugal' for its cathedrals, churches, library and university.

ALGARVE (FARO/LOULÉ)

After the European Championship is over, this 30,000 all-new stadium will be transformed into a multi-purpose athletics arena. It is located between the municipalities of Faro and Loulé in Portugal's most popular tourist region, and it is close to a choice of golden beaches as well as orange groves, golf courses and beautiful villages. Faro also has its own airport.

D. AFONSO HENRIQUES (GUIMARÃES)

Guimarães is known as the city where Portugal was born. It was the country's first capital and is now home to 160,000 people. The stadium, named after Portugal's first king, is an increased-capacity reconstruction of Vitória Sport Club's home ground. It was the first of all the ten stadiums to be completed – ahead of schedule – in June 2003.

DR MAGALHÃES PESSOA (LEIRIA)

Based in Leiria, a city between Coimbra and Lisbon in the centre of Portugal, the capacity of this remodelled stadium has been increased from 11,000 to 30,000 by building three new seating areas. Leiria is famous for its pine forest – the oldest in the country. Despite its industrial background, it is a beautiful city set amongst rolling hills.

JOSÉ ALVALADE (LISBON)

Home of Sporting Lisbon, this modern 52,000-capacity stadium is a fitting venue for international football. Located right next to Sporting's old ground, it is part of a large complex that includes shops, restaurants and even houses. One of Europe's sunniest and oldest capitals, Lisbon is a lively and varied city to visit.

LUZ (LISBON)

This new 65,000-capacity stadium has been built on land adjacent to Benfica's famous old ground and given the same name. It will host the Euro 2004 final, in the club's centenary year. In English 'luz' means 'light', earning the previous stadium the nickname Stadium of Light (which was then 'borrowed' by Sunderland). But in fact Luz is the area in which the stadium is located. Benfica fans have dubbed the ground the 'New Cathedral', while UEFA call it the 'jewel of Euro 2004'.

Tournament Rules

Here is some vital information about how the tournament works, plus a few unusual rules you probably never knew. And will probably never need to!

Fair Play

All teams and players are asked to:

Play their very best

Entertain supporters

Avoid arguments with referees

Show self-control

Be humble in defeat

Respect players

Set a good example to children

France won the Euro 2000 Fair Play award after just eight bookings in the tournament, which they won.

The 'Silver Goal' Rule

If two teams finish the 90 minutes level (only in the quarter-finals, semi-finals and final) then extra time is played. If one team scores more than the other in the first 15 minute period of extra time, then they win the game. Otherwise, a second 15-minute period is played. If neither team can outscore the other during that period, then the match is decided by penalties.

Getting ahead of the group

If two or more teams are level at the end of the group stage, this is how to work out which team goes through:

1	Points won in the games between the teams in question
2	Goal difference in the games between the teams in question
3	Goals scored in the games between the teams in question
4	Goal difference in the overall group
5	Goals scored in all group games
6	Co-efficient from 2002 World Cup and Euro 2004 qualifying games
7	'Fair Play' rating at Euro 2004
8	Drawing of lots

Golden Boot Winners

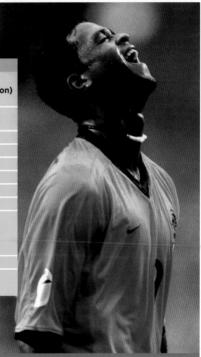

(Top scorers of final tournaments only)	
1960	Hautte (France) Ivanov, Ponedelnik (both Soviet Union) Galic, Jerkovic (both Yugoslavia) 2
1964	Pereda (Spain) Bene, Novák (both Hungary) 2
1968	Dzajic (Yugoslavia) 2
1972	G Müller (West Germany) 4
1976	D Müller (West Germany) 4
1980	Allofs (West Germany) 3
1984	Platini (France) 9
1988	Van Basten (Holland) 5
1992	Bergkamp (Holland) Brolin (Sweden) Riedle (Germany) Larsen (Denmark) 4
1996	Shearer (England) 5
2000	Kluivert (Holland) Milosevic (Yugoslavia) 6

Did you know?

Players' names on the back of their shirts cannot exceed 7.5cm in height.

Article 22.02 in the tournament rules states 'Doping is forbidden.'

Only one of the 16 teams at Euro 2004 is allowed to play in Portugal during the month before the tournament starts. And that's Portugal.

If a team refuses to play, they are automatically disqualified.

The losing semi-finalists receive a diploma, but the losing finalists are given a plaque.

According to UEFA rules, teams must arrive in the venue city on the evening before the match, at the latest.

All stadium clocks must be stopped at 45 and 90 minutes, even if the match is still being played.

The Trophy

It was Henri Delaunay, the first ever Secretary General of UEFA and former secretary of the French Football Federation, who came up with the idea of the European Championship back in 1927. Delaunay (along with Jules Rimet) also started the World Cup, but he died before the first qualifying competition eventually got under way in 1958. The trophy still bears his name, however. Winning teams are not allowed to keep the original silver trophy – which is 50cm tall and weighs 10kg – but instead get an exact replica.

Meet the teams

Group A

Portugal

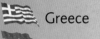
Greece

Spain

Russia

Group B

France

England

Switzerland

Croatia

Group C

Sweden

Bulgaria

Denmark

Italy

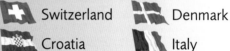

SWEDEN

LATVIA

DENMARK

HOLLAND

ENGLAND

GERMANY

CZECH REP.

SWITZ.

FRANCE

CROATIA

BULGARIA

ITALY

PORTUGAL

GREECE

SPAIN

Group D

Czech Rep.

Latvia

Germany

Holland

R U S S I A

Russia has the highest population of any nation in Europe – 144.5 million. **Latvia** is smallest with 2.3 million. Russia also has more neighbours than anyone else – 14. They are Azerbaijan, Belarus, China, Estonia, Finland, Georgia, Kazakhstan, Latvia, Lithuania, Mongolia, North Korea, Norway, Poland and Ukraine.

The English have many things to thank the Swedes for – Abba, Svennis (that's Sven-Goran Eriksson to us), saunas and Ikea to name but a few. There's also a lot of footballers!

Bulgaria famously finished third in the 1994 World Cup, which was held in the USA. The team beat Germany in the quarter-final and was led by the legendary forward Hristo Stoichkov. He is Bulgaria's greatest ever player, and he only recently announced his decision to retire.

There are four native languages spoken in **Spain** – Castilian Spanish, Basque, Catalan and Galician.

Portugal's 'Golden Generation' – nearly a whole team of talented young players – was discovered in the late 1980s by Carlos Queiroz – formerly Sir Alex Ferguson's No. 2 at Manchester United and currently Real Madrid manager. The team, featuring amongst others Luis Figo, Fernando Couto and Rui Costa, won the World Under-20s Championship in 1989 and 1991. Euro 2004 is their farewell tournament.

Group A

Portugal

Greece

Spain

Russia

Portugal

The host nation might not have had any competitive matches to prepare for this tournament (they qualified automatically) but confidence will be high. They have immense talent throughout the squad and, as ever, will try to play attacking, stylish football. With either Pauleta or Nuno Gomes up front, Portugal pose a dangerous threat to goal. And with the great Luis Figo supporting them from the right, as well as promising youngsters like Cristiano Ronaldo (Manchester Utd) and Hugo Viana (Newcastle), scoring opportunities should come thick and fast.

The problem is in defence. Although the experience of Jorge Costa (Porto) and Fernando Couto (Lazio, pictured) will be useful, they are vulnerable against pace. Both veteran centrebacks are also prone to the occasional rash challenge. If they are to progress to the tournament's latter stages goalkeeper Vitor Baia (Porto) must stay on his toes.

Coach Luiz Felipe Scolari – known as 'Big Phil' – will keep the midfield tight even though fans demand attacking football. Scolari won the 2002 World Cup with Brazil, so he should know what he's doing!

Greece

Greece opened their Euro 2004 qualifying campaign with two losses but staged an amazing comeback to win their group ahead of Spain. Their success came from a strong defensive record – they sometimes play with five at the back. Stylianos Venetidis and Leicester City centre-back Nikos Dabizas are the likely pairing at the heart of that defensive wall. Another player who used to earn his wages in England is former Leicester City midfielder Theo Zagorakis, who holds everything together in the centre of the pitch.

Greece, coached by German Otto Rehhagel, use a pressing game to harry opponents off the ball, which is the most effective way of upsetting the flowing rhythm of teams like Portugal and Spain.

There is another familiar face in Stylianos Giannakopoulos, the Bolton Wanderers star who can play on the right wing or in support of the lone striker – Vryzas or Charisteas, while veteran playmaker Vassilios Tsartas might feature as well.

Greece have only played at two major tournaments before – the European Championship in 1980 and the 1994 World Cup and did not win a match at either.

Spain

Individually, Spain's players are as good as any nation's in this tournament, but there are always question marks hanging over the team when the pressure is on – they could win Euro 2004, or will they slip up yet again?

Their qualifying campaign was mixed. They started brilliantly, but a poor 0–0 draw with Northern Ireland opened a gap for Greece to take the top spot in the group. Spain then saw off Norway with ease in the play-offs.

In Portugal, they have the opportunity for revenge against the Greeks, and the 'local derby' with the hosts should also be an exciting event.

With Casillas in goal, Puyol and Helguera in the centre of defence, Salgado on the right and Juanito on the left, Spain have a very good defensive line. Ruben Baraja is the team's heartbeat in midfield, with Vicente (right) charging down the right side of the field, Exteberria down the left, and Valeron in the middle. Opponents don't know where the danger is coming from. The star, of course, is Spain's top scorer of all time – Raul.

At Euro 2000, Spain were beaten by Norway 1–0 but then beat Yugoslavia 4–3 in the most amazing game of the competition. They were then knocked out by France in a hotly-contested quarter-final, during which Raul missed a vital penalty.

Russia

Russia looked mediocre during their play-off game against Wales in Moscow (0–0) but then travelled to Cardiff and earned qualification with a good 1–0 win. They will have to play a lot better in Portugal though, if they are to progress from Group A.

The central defenders Sergei Ignashevitch and Victor Onopko, however, make a formidable barrier and the full backs Sennikov and Evseev (who both play for Lokomotiv Moscow) are quietly effective.

In midfield, Chelsea's Aleksei Smertin (on loan at Portsmouth this season) is a tough-tackling player who irritates opponents and occasionally looks like he can dominate games.

Alexander Mostovoi, and Dmitri Loskov are excellent creative players who can unlock any door. Mostovoi in particular has proved his class during his club career in Spain with Celta Vigo.

Up front, Dmitri Bulykin is strong and tall, supported by the excellent Dmitri Sychev of Marseille. Roland Gusev is dangerous from the right, and young star Marat Izmailov charges in from the left with amazing pace to cause chaos in the penalty box.

Coach Georgi Yartsev hopes his hit-and-miss side finds the consistency to fulfil their potential.

Group B

France

England

Switzerland

Croatia

France

After the disappointment of the 2002 World Cup, France are more determined than ever to win this competition. Which is bad news for everyone else because France have undoubtedly the most talented team at Euro 2004 and are most people's favourites to win. Last November they set a national record of 13 consecutive wins by demolishing Germany 3–0 – in Germany!

The key to their success is hardly a secret – they've got all the best players! Zinedine Zidane (Real Madrid) is the headline act, while around him in midfield Patrick Vieira, Robert Pires (both Arsenal) and Claude Makelele (Chelsea) form a terrifying combination.

The defence is equally awesome. They have a decade of medal-winning experience in Lilian Thuram (Juventus) and Bixente Lizarazu (Bayern Munich) on the right and left respectively. In the centre, Manchester United's Mikael Silvestre has earned a starting place, supported from the bench by Auxerre's brilliant Philippe Mexes and Rangers new boy Jean-Alain Boumsong.

This is the last tournament for ageing captain Marcel Desailly of Chelsea, while keeper Gregory Coupet (Lyon) has replaced out-of-favour Fabien Barthez (Manchester United) effortlessly.

Up front, the pin-up boys Thierry Henry (Arsenal) and David Trezeguet (Juventus) could end up competing against each other to become top scorer in Portugal.

England

France have never beaten England in a major tournament, but they did win a friendly at Wembley in 1999 thanks to two goals from Nicolas Anelka (now at Manchester City). The most recent meeting was in 2000, a 1–1 draw in Paris in which Michael Owen scored and Paul Scholes (left) played.

There is no doubt that England have many of the world's best players, but whether they can be moulded into a trophy-winning team is what English fans are waiting to find out on June 13.

Victory over Switzerland and Croatia should be well within England's capabilities, so there is an awful lot riding on the opening game against the reigning European champions. As France's Patrick

Vieira commented, 'Anybody can beat anybody. There are only three games in the group, so the first three points are important.'

Sven-Goran Eriksson's reaction when France's name was pulled from the hat alongside England was, "Very, very nice. Beautiful." Maybe he was a little shocked.

Switzerland

It has been suggested that Switzerland only won their qualifying group because the Republic of Ireland and Russia messed things up. While there might be a grain of truth in that, the Swiss do possess the skill to cause one or two upsets at Euro 2004.

Switzerland have much to thank the Yakin family for. Not only is Murat Yakin the most important defender in the national side, but his brother Hakan is the side's biggest creative weapon. He will lurk behind the strikers, looking for the killer pass and maybe even bag a few goals for himself. He has already proved himself in the Champions League with Swiss club Basle.

Also in midfield is the tricky Raphael Wicky, who one day can look like the best player in the world, and the next look like he's never seen a football before in his life!

Coach Jakob 'Kobi' Kuhn will be concerned that his side has a tendency to concede a lot of goals, which might mean that Liverpool's defender Stephane Henchoz returns to the starting line-up in place of Patrick Muller. Despite the handful of familiar names and the dangerous young/old strike partnership of Alex Frei/Stephane Chapuisat, Switzerland will probably be battling for third place with Croatia.

Croatia

The current team may not be as naturally gifted as the side that finished third in the 1998 World Cup, but it is defensively solid and has some potential match winners.

At the back, Robert Kovac plays for Bayern Munich, Igor Tudor for Juventus, Dario Simic for AC Milan and Boris Zivkovic plays for Portsmouth.

Left-sided midfielder Milan Rapaic, who plays for Turkish club Fenerbahce, is inconsistent but on his day can rival anyone for inventiveness and goal threat from the wing. The likes of Srna, Rosso, Babic, Leko and Niko Kovac (Robert's younger brother) do not compare with the 1990s partnership of Boban, Prosinecki and Asanovic but they play good, simple football and are mentally strong.

With Dado Prso (pictured right) and Ivica Mornar playing up front, the tactic should be to cross the ball as often as possible because both forwards are powerful but not technically brilliant.

However, when Ivica Olic is playing, Croatia can step up a level and pose a serious challenge. Olic is quick and skilful – surely a star of the future.

In their qualifying group, Croatia were clearly not as good as Bulgaria, but did well to hold off Belgium in the race for second place. Croatia are almost always at major tournaments but a repeat of their 1998 heroics is unlikely.

Group C

Sweden

Bulgaria

Denmark

Italy

Sweden

Sweden's defeat at the hands of surprise package Latvia in the last qualifying game last autumn brought to an end an amazing unbeaten run in all qualifiers stretching back to 1997. But winning qualifiers is no use if you can't win at the tournament – and at Euro 2000 they didn't win a game and only scored twice. The 2002 World Cup was better, and Sweden topped a group that contained England, Argentina and Nigeria, only to be knocked out in the second round by Senegal. Maybe 2004 will be different.

Their form in qualifying meant they are among the favourites to win the tournament, but the reality is different. When they were drawn in a group with Bulgaria, Denmark and Italy, there was a negative reaction back home. The Swedish media doesn't believe the national team can perform when they are favourites – although they will have their work cut out to beat Italy, who only lost Euro 2000's final to a golden goal.

Sweden have a solid defence led by the country's 2003 Player of the Year, Olof Mellberg of Aston Villa, and Southampton's Michael Svensson. The midfield relies on the forward runs of Fredrik Ljungberg (Arsenal) and Anders Svensson (Southampton). Up front, the fiery young Zlatan Ibrahimovic (Ajax) is the player that opposition defenders will be watching, and that may open up extra space for the experienced Marcus Allback of Aston Villa.

Bulgaria

Bulgaria's approach to Euro 2004 should be simple: give the ball to Dimitar Berbatov. The Bayer Leverkusen striker is a tall, powerful goal poacher who is difficult to stop.

Some fans might argue that Celtic playmaker Stilian Petrov (left) is the star. Indeed, Petrov is the kind of player who plays better at international level than he does at club level. But the midfield maestro – captain of this young team – needs to show the ability to carry his side when it is under pressure.

Marian Hristov plays his club football in Germany with Kaiserslautern, while Georgi Peev is a star at Ukrainian superpower Dynamo Kiev, and Wolfsburg winger Martin

Petrov works hard and scores goals.

Bulgaria, a mix of spirit and stability, did well to qualify from their group ahead of Croatia and Belgium. But Euro 2004 might have come too early for this side to emulate Bulgaria's stars of the 1994 World Cup, where they finished third.

Denmark

The Danes possess perhaps the most dangerous weapon in top level football – pace. With PSV Eindhoven's Dennis Rommedahl and Chelsea's Jesper Gronkjaer on the wings, they have a lightning quick attacking line-up.

The target man is Ebbe Sand of German giants Schalke, while former Newcastle United failure Jon Dahl Tomasson is also dangerous. He now plays for AC Milan and cleverly finds space in and around the penalty box. He scores a goal every two international games on average.

The experience of midfield captain Morten Weighorst, and defenders Martin Laursen and Thomas Helveg will be important, as will the muscle of Everton's Thomas Gravesen and the attacking flair of Martin Jorgensen (right). But Denmark are not as good going back as they are in attack, making their counter-attacking style risky.

Goalkeeper Thomas Sorensen is no Peter Schmeichel (the ex-Manchester United legend who used to play for Denmark) but neither is he the worst 'keeper at the tournament. This team is capable of outscoring most of the sides in this group but will have to remain organized.

Italy

The Euro 2000 runners-up are led by Italy's most successful club coach ever – Giovanni Trapattoni. They are not only the favourites to win Group C, but are also expected to reach at least the semi-finals.

Key defender Alessandro Nesta believes they threw away the chance to win the 2002 World Cup (they were dumped out by co-hosts South Korea) and he and the rest of the team are determined to make up for lost time. In Francesco Totti (Roma) and Alessandro Del Piero (Juventus), they possess two of the world's most gifted and creative players. The prolific Inter Milan star Christian Vieri completes a deadly attacking trio, with the tricky 'Pippo' Inzaghi in reserve alongside super-sub Marco Di Vaio.

Apart from Mauro Camoranesi, Italy do not have many wingers to choose from, so the midfield is made up of gritty central midfielders like Cristiano Zanetti.

If opponents manage to get past the midfield they have to contend with the best central defensive partnership in the world – Nesta and Inter's Fabio Cannavaro. And then there is Gianluigi Buffon – the world's most expensive 'keeper who cost Juventus £33m. If Italy can contain the fast wingers of Denmark in their opening game, they should go on to win the group.

Group D

Czech Rep.

Latvia

Germany

Holland

Czech Republic

When Group D was drawn, the Czech Republic went from being one of the favourites to win Euro 2004 to not even being sure of winning their group.

In last year's qualifying stages, they pipped Holland to an automatic place, so the Dutch will be out for revenge. And 2002 World Cup finalists Germany know how to win while playing badly. It's a blow for the Czechs, who often suffer from a lack of confidence.

With Pavel Nedved and Karel Poborsky (left) in their side, though, they still have a chance. Juventus' left-sided playmaker Nedved is one of the best players in Europe. This is the last chance for Poborsky – now playing for Sparta Prague in the Czech Republic – to repeat his form at Euro 96, which led to Manchester United buying him.

In the centre, Tomas Rosicky is brilliant: fast, intelligent and full of ideas. He could be the man to get the ball to giant centre-forward Jan Koller, a massive man with great first touch. Team-mates at German club Borussia Dortmund, they have formed a good understanding. Liverpool's Milan Baros might be called on if the goals dry up.

Latvia

The 2004 European Championship is the first major tournament that Latvia – the small ex-Baltic state – has qualified for.

Their defence, marshalled by Arsenal's Igors Stepanovs, will come under intense pressure from the likes of Holland's Ruud van Nistelrooy. In qualifying for the finals, Latvia proved to be a good counter-attacking side, and they could even have topped their group instead of Sweden.

But when they kick off in Euro 2004's Group of Death, they will be up against a different class of opposition. Coach Alexandrs Starkovs will stick to a 4–4–2 formation and hope central midfielders like Valentins Lobanovs, Jurijs Laizans and Vitalis Astafjevs can harry and hurry opponents into making mistakes. Imants Bleidelis on the right and Andrejs Rubins on the left are crucial to Latvia's hopes of getting the ball forward to the prolific Maris Verpakovskis and Southampton's Marian Pahars.

The fact that they managed to beat Turkey – third in the 2002 World Cup – to reach Portugal will give them hope, but confidence is a fragile thing and Latvia's could quickly be shattered.

Germany

For the last few years, Germany have not been able to find any decent strikers, but that's changed now. Stuttgart forward Kevin Kuranyi could add a new, fresh dimension to Germany's usually dull style of play.

This is a team that knows how to get to finals. They made it to the 2002 World Cup final despite not playing particularly well during that tournament. And these days they play a direct, forceful game.

The midfield will be powerful and hard-working. Playing alongside Michael Ballack are Jens Jeremies and Bernd Schneider, both ferocious tacklers. Jeremies will try to dominate the centre of the pitch, while Schneider will make intelligent forward runs. If Ballack's Bayern team-mate Sebastien Diesler is fit, he adds much-needed creativity.

The German defence is held together by experienced players like Marko Rehmer, Carsten Ramelow, Christian Worns and Jens Novotny, with younger stars like Sebastien Kehl and Christoph Metzelder eager for a chance. None of them is considered the best in the world, but with a goalkeeper as good as Oliver Kahn of Bayern Munich behind them, that shouldn't matter.

You can never write the German team off, and this time they're seeking their fourth European Championship.

Holland

When Dutch players get together on international duty, it is anybody's guess what may happen on the pitch. Sometimes they play brilliantly and win, and sometimes they don't. When everyone is happy though, the Dutch possess a squad to rival the best.

This could be the last hurrah for the 'old guard' of Frank De Boer, Jaap Stam (right), Edwin Van Der Sar, Edgar Davids, Clarence Seedorf, Marc Overmars and Phillip Cocu. All of them are excellent players who have had remarkable club careers and this is their chance to go out with a bang internationally.

The new generation includes brilliant winger Andy Van Der Meyde and midfield hero Rafael Van Der Vaart – and they are every bit as good as the stars they are replacing.

Ever since losing to Germany in the 1974 World Cup final, there has been an intense rivalry between the two nations who will be meeting in the Group of Death. Holland have the edge in terms of pure talent, but can they can match the teamwork and composure of Germany in their opening match? Group games don't come any bigger than this!

Thierry Henry

Country | France   **Position** | Striker   **Date of Birth** | 17.08.1977   **Club** | Arsenal

Born in Paris almost 27 years ago, Thierry Daniel Henry's first club was Monaco, in the glamorous principality in the south of France.

He made his debut in August of 1994 but the visiting side, Nice, won 2–0. Just seven more games followed for Henry that season, and he scored three goals, but a few years later he was the hottest property in world football.

France's top scorer at the 1998 World Cup – in which he played as a right winger – and again at Euro 2000, his performances in the blue shirt of France have been as spectacular as his form for Arsenal.

Apart from an unhappy six month spell at Juventus in Italy in the second half of the 1998–99 season, Henry's career has been a tale of constant improvement. In fact, if he gets any better, defenders are going to start thinking about a change of career.

Arsenal boss Arsene Wenger has been vital to Henry's success. As Monaco manager, Wenger signed the young winger and nurtured his talents as he captained France's Under–18s side, was named Young Footballer of the Year in 1996 and then broke into the senior side.

Wenger knew that he had a very special player on his hands and years later, when Henry's move to Juventus turned sour, the manager took him to Highbury for just £10.5 million – a genuine bargain. Wenger turned Henry from a winger into a striker and he has not stopped scoring since his move to London.

Indeed, he has tired of scoring 20+ goals per season for the club that he loves so dearly, and now aims for 30+. No-one in the global game is quicker and no-one has as many tricks in front of goal. Be afraid. A cross between: Ronaldo and a greyhound.

Raul

Country | Spain **Position** | Striker **Date of Birth** | 27.06.1977 **Club** | Real Madrid, Spain

You may think that Raul is Real Madrid through and through. But in truth he grew up in an Atletico Madrid supporting family and from the age of 13 played in their youth team.

It was only when Atletico shut down their youth system to save money that Raul moved to Real, and started a journey that saw him become a legend.

He began the 1994–95 season in Real's C team, scoring 13 goals in his first seven games. Then, after one game for the B team, became the youngest player ever to play in the first team, aged 17 years and four months. It was even more impressive considering the man he knocked out of the team – Emilio Butragueno, was considered by some to be the best Spanish player of all time.

On the international stage, things have been less convincing. Despite being Spain's top goal scorer ever, Raul has not come close to winning any silverware with his country. He was ignored for Euro 96, and made his debut after the tournament, against the Czech Republic. And, despite playing brilliantly in the qualifiers for Euro 2000 as well as the 1998 and 2002 World Cups, he disappointed once the competitions began. Maybe this year it will be different.

At Real Madrid, the trophies have been easier to come by. In fact, by the time you read this he may have overtaken Alfredo di Stefano as the top scorer in the Champions League (or the European Cup, as it used to be called). Di Stefano had 49, but Raul is catching him quickly. It's amazing to think that he is so young – he'll be 27 during the summer of 2004.

He is married to a Spanish model, and many see Raul as Spain's answer to David Beckham. A cross between: Zidane, Van Nistelrooy, Del Piero and Di Stefano.

Pavel Nedved

Country | Czech Rep. **Position** | Midfielder **Date of Birth** | 30.08.1972 **Club** | Juventus, Italy

The European Footballer of the Year and Zinedine Zidane's replacement at Juventus, is only two months younger than the Frenchman. But his limitless energy make him seem 21, not 31.

Nedved charges around the pitch like a more talented version of Robbie Savage (and apparently goes to the same hairdresser too!) and his desire has taken the Czech Republic to Euro 2004.

If he had been born a couple of miles further east, Nedved would have been German but he was born in Cheb, a small town in the north east of the Czech Republic and started his career as a striker at FC Marila Pribram. He moved to Czech giants Sparta Prague in 1992.

After Euro 96, PSV Eindhoven wanted to buy the talented Nedved, who is equally at home on both sides of the pitch. He has a diploma in geometry and once wanted to be an accountant. But at that time Lazio were spending money like it was going out of fashion (no jokes about signing Czechs, please!) and convinced the midfielder to move to Italy.

Before the 1999–2000 season, Lazio manager Sven-Goran Eriksson put his squad through intense training, at the end of which Nedved was the only player left standing. That season the Czech star inspired the side to its first ever league and cup double. Then, in 2001, Juventus gave Lazio £26m for his services and he has proved to be worth every penny.

Known as the Czech Cannon or The Rocket for his blazing long-range goals, his committed and inspirational performances for club and country resulted in him being given the 2003 FIFA European Footballer of the Year award ahead of Zidane and Thierry Henry.

A cross between: Robbie Savage and Thierry Henry.

Luis Figo

Country | Portugal **Position** | Midfielder **Date of Birth** | 04.11.1972 **Club** | Real Madrid, Spain

This is goodbye for Luis Filipe Madeira Caeiro Figo. He intends to retire from international football following Euro 2004 and he will be sadly missed.

For over a decade, Figo has been one of the world's most skilful players, a winger who leaves opponents trailing in his wake. One of Portugal's famous 'Golden Generation' that also includes Rui Costa and Joao Pinto, he made his international debut against Luxembourg just before his 19th birthday in 1991 and Euro 2004 will see him win his 100th cap.

Born in the working class Almada district of Lisbon, Figo joined Sporting Lisbon aged 11 and got into the first team in 1989. He became world champion with Portugal's youth side the same year and again in 1991. He became captain of Sporting in 1994, aged just 23.

At club level, Figo is used to controversy. Before the 1995–96 season he signed pre-contract agreements with both Juventus and Parma and so FIFA banned him from moving to Italy for two years. That was good news for Barcelona, who snapped him up for just £1.2m. After winning league and cup titles with Barça, he switched to their hated rivals Real Madrid in 2000. The £37m price tag was then a world record but Barça fans have never forgiven him.

He is now managed at Real by Carlos Queiroz, the same man who gave him his international debut all those years ago. Portugal, despite their brilliant attacking football, have never quite hit the heights that some people thought they would over the last decade. At Euro 96 they reached the quarter-final, and four years later made it to the semi-final. Luis Figo will be dreaming of going one better this time around. The former World and European Footballer of the Year wants to go out with a bang.

A cross between: Ryan Giggs and David Beckham.

Michael Ballack

Country | Germany   **Position** | Midfielder   **Date of Birth** | 26.09.1976   **Club** | Bayern Munich

At the 2002 World Cup, Michael Ballack wore the Number 13 shirt and his luck was mixed.

In the semi-final he scored the winning goal against South Korea, but he also picked up a booking that meant he would miss the final against Brazil. Germany had little chance of beating Brazil anyway, but without their best player they were doomed.

The Germans are sometimes criticised for being too defensive and for not producing players with creativity. However, Ballack has the vision of David Beckham, the well-timed runs into the penalty box of Freddie Ljungberg and the long legs of Patrick Vieira to help in the tackle.

Before the World Cup he played at Bayer Leverkusen and led the unfancied club to the 2002 Champions League final – where they lost to Real Madrid – and also to second place in the Bundesliga. Earlier in his career, he won the league with Kaiserslautern.

The great Franz Beckenbauer claimed he was the best midfielder in Europe. So it was with great relief that fans saw him fulfil his enormous potential at the last World Cup and then move to Bayern Munich, where he should go on to win a sackful of medals.

There is only a handful of players who can totally control the pace of a game. Roy Keane is one, Zinedine Zidane another. And Michael Ballack is in that category too.

A cross between: Roy Keane, Patrick Vieira, Fredrik Ljungberg, David Beckham, Franz Beckenbauer.

Zinedine Zidane

Country | France **Position** | Midfielder **Date of Birth** | 23.06.1972 **Club** | Real Madrid, Spain

Of all the superstars at Real Madrid, the most glamorous club in the world, Zidane shines the brightest.

The French genius will go down in history as one of the all-time greats, a player so talented he stands out from the rest. Zidane, born in France of Algerian parents, began his career in 1988 when he was spotted by talent scouts from French club Cannes during a trial at a football academy. After four seasons, and despite an offer from his hometown club Marseille, Zidane joined Bordeaux and stayed for four years.

In 1996 'Zizou' was bought by Juventus, the Italian club known as the 'Old Lady'. He started winning medals. Lots of medals. He was voted 1998 European Footballer of the Year and World Footballer of the Year in 1998, 2000 and again in 2004. He became the world's most expensive player in 2001, following his £46m transfer to Real Madrid. At Real he famously scored an amazing goal to win the 2002 Champions League, confirming his reputation as a man who loves performing on the big stage.

The 6ft 1in playmaker scored two headed goals to win the 1998 World Cup Final and also inspired France to glory at Euro 2000. A brilliant attacking midfielder, he drifts all over the pitch during games and has more tricks up his sleeve than a magician in a joke shop. That explains why he is the most popular man in France.

Zidane will have his 32nd birthday during Euro 2004 and could celebrate by winning yet another medal to add to his collection.

A cross between: Michel Platini and God.

Ruud van Nistelrooy

Country | Holland   **Position** | Striker   **Date of Birth** | 01.07.1976   **Club** | Manchester United

Van Nistelrooy once boasted, 'Defenders never know what I'm going to do.' But that's not true – everyone knows what he's going to do. Van Nistelrooy simply puts the ball in the net. In fact, he scores so freely it's a wonder that defenders bother trying to stop him at all.

The Old Trafford superhero had a tiff with Holland coach Dick Advocaat last year about being substituted, but by the time the opening clash with Germany arrives in June 2004, that will be a distant memory.

Holland's only problem is that van Nistelrooy and his team-mate Patrick Kluivert are too similar. They were born on the same day –July 1, 1976 – are both the same height – 1.88m – and play in the penalty area. Kluivert is Holland's most prolific striker in history (with over 40), while van Nistelrooy is currently the world's greatest goalscorer. Advocaat will probably play them both and it's van Nistelrooy's chance to eclipse not only Kluivert but also Dennis Bergkamp and Marco van Basten as Holland's best ever striker.

Patrick Kluivert

Country | Holland   **Position** | Striker   **Date of Birth** | 01.07.1976   **Club** | Barcelona, Spain

No-one has scored as many goals for Holland as Kluivert. His club, Barcelona, may not be winning many trophies, but that has not stopped the goals flowing at international level. However, recently Kluivert was dropped to accommodate Ruud van Nistelrooy, and the Manchester United player blew Scotland away with a hat-trick. On the pitch, things haven't always gone smoothly and when Kluivert moved from Ajax to Milan he lost his form before moving to Barcelona in 1998. But in 2000 he was joint top scorer at the European Championship in Belgium/Holland and is once again considered to be one of the game's deadliest predators.

He gets more assists than van Nistelrooy as he opens space for team-mates, and finds them with clever head-downs and lay-offs. At Euro 2000 he netted six goals – how many this time?

Alexander Mostovoi

Country | Russia   **Position** | Midfielder   **Date of Birth** | 22.08.1968   **Club** | Celta Vigo, Spain

Mostovoi has been in more trouble with the Russian authorities than James Bond. The temperamental midfielder has been dropped from the national team many times over the years following public rows with coaches.

Now approaching his 36th birthday, he will have to curb his fiery side and knuckle down to some hard work as Russia hope to upset the applecart in Group A. The veteran playmaker is the ideas man at the heart of the Russian midfield. With younger players doing most of the running, Mostovoi will be able to concentrate on finding his best form – and it can be spectacular. He has played as sweeper for Russia in the past but this summer they need his brilliance in attack.

David Trézéguet

Country | France   **Position** | Striker   **Date of Birth** | 15.10.1977   **Club** | Juventus, Italy

Born in France but raised in Argentina, David Nazareno Trézéguet started his career at Argentine club Platense in 1993. By 1995 he had relocated to France and began making a name for himself, together with Thierry Henry, at Monaco. After scoring the winner against Italy in the Euro 2000 final, he joined Juventus for £15m to play alongside many of the international defenders he had just humiliated. At Juve, his goalscoring ratio has been awesome, eclipsing even Alessandro Del Piero.

He may not have the skills of Henry but defenders cannot take their eyes off this France 98 winner for a second. Not because he's blessed with such good looks, but because if he finds an inch of space in the box, he'll score.

Alessandro Del Piero

Country | Italy   **Position** | Striker   **Date of Birth** | 09.11.1974   **Club** | Juventus, Italy

Italy's Golden Boy is now a man. He was once the world's best-paid footballer and fans expected him to become the world's best too.

Troubled by injury and exhaustion, however, he has disappointed them. A veteran of Euro 96, France 98, Euro 2000 and Japan/Korea 2002, he has never shown his true genius on the international stage.

At the age of 29, it's about time he showed his dribbling and shooting skills to the world. If not, fans might give up on the Golden Boy who would be king.

Patrick Vieira

Country | France   **Position** | Midfielder   **Date of Birth** | 23.06.1976   **Club** | Arsenal

The Arsenal captain is taller than a lamp-post, stronger than a rhino and as skilful as a very, very skilful thing. The French powerhouse has been in London since 1996 – in fact Arsene Wenger demanded the Gunners should buy the midfielder from AC Milan (£4m) before he would accept the manager's job.

Wenger's judgement proved correct and Vieira has been Arsenal's most important player ever since. His value was shown at the end of the 2002-03 season. Injury forced him to watch from the sidelines as his team-mates threw away the title. He'll have plenty more opportunities to win trophies in England, though, having signed a contract that keeps him at Arsenal until 2007.

Vieira is perhaps the best defensive midfielder in the world. His tackling and passing skills keep Arsenal and France one step ahead of the rest, allowing Zidane and Henry to focus on performing their magic in attack. Playing alongside Chelsea's Claude Makelele means he can also surge forward on one of his devastating runs, causing panic amongst opposition ranks.

The phrase 'midfield general' might have been invented for Patrick Vieira.

Jan Koller

Country | Czech Republic **Position** | Striker **Date of Birth** | 30.03.1973 **Club** | Borussia Dortmund, Germany

Koller makes England's rugby captain Martin Johnson look like a big girl's blouse. He's enormous. And he's got the skill of Zidane to match... OK, that's an exaggeration, but for such a tall striker, Koller's first touch is excellent. He often finds himself playing up front alone for the Czech Republic. But even by himself he can either hold the ball up or blast a shot away in the twinkling of an eye.

His 6 ft 8 ins frame simply batters opponents out of the way. But the Czechs prefer to play the ball on the ground and only hoof it onto his head when things are getting desperate.

He made a goalscoring international debut in 1999 and hasn't stopped since. Embarrassed not to qualify for the 2002 World Cup, he'll be fired up for success. Half bulldozer, half ballerina!

Jon Dahl Tomasson

Country | Denmark **Position** | Striker **Date of Birth** | 29.08.1976 **Club** | AC Milan, Italy

In 1997, both Barcelona and Ajax wanted to buy Tomasson from Dutch side Heerenveen. But he chose Newcastle instead and things didn't go well at all – he only scored 3 goals in 23 games.

Thankfully, after that bad experience, he's now back at the top. After Newcastle, a transfer back to Holland with Feyenoord, where he won the 2002 UEFA Cup, earned him a big-money move to Milan. The Danish international is not a prolific forward; he lacks the strength of his team-mate Ebbe Sand and he isn't particularly quick. But he does possess the element of surprise. Just when defenders think he must have been substituted, he pops up out of nowhere and lashes home a spectacular goal.

Francesco Totti

Country | Italy   **Position** | Striker   **Date of Birth** | 27.09.1976   **Club** | Roma, Italy

The darling of Roma fans, and pin-up of Italy's top league, Serie A, Totti is beautiful in two ways. His good looks make women fall to their knees, while his bewildering array of tricks with a football leave defenders humiliated and on their backsides.

His career with Roma started way back in 1992 and he has developed into the most consistently creative player in Italy. Competition comes from Alessandro Del Piero and it is difficult to find room for both stars in the international line-up.

Totti is not a penalty box forward and he spends much of his time dropping deep to find space in front of the midfield. He has never scored more than 15 goals in a season, but goals are not what Totti is all about. Vieri and Inzaghi are the goal machines of the team, and Totti is the operator. Without his vision, the Italian team struggles to get the ball forward with any imagination and grinds to a halt.

Totti enjoyed Euro 2000 and at the 2002 World Cup he was preferred to Del Piero, playing behind Vieri. Giovanni Trapattoni, Italy's manager, might be tempted to play all three superstars this summer.

Juan Carlos Valeron

Country | Spain   Position | Midfielder   Date of Birth | 16.06.1975   Club | Deportivo La Coruña, Spain

One of the least appreciated geniuses in the global game, Valeron's talents have been somewhat hidden behind those of his team-mate Raul. But Valeron is a potential match-winner who is capable of taking Raul's place in the Spain line-up or playing alongside him.

He is at his best 'in the hole' behind the strikers but can easily float around the pitch, marauding along the flanks or surging into the penalty box. He doesn't score many goals, but his game is all about creating chances for others.

Few European players can match Valeron's technique and his instinctive feel for playing attractive, attacking football. He started at Las Palmas in 1994 before joining Real Mallorca, then Atletico Madrid. Following Euro 2000, where he played in two group games, he was snapped up by title-chasing Deportivo La Coruña, where he has become an important player in an exciting team.

A few years ago he was compared to Zinedine Zidane in the Spanish press, and Euro 2004 is his chance to prove they weren't barking up the wrong tree. An energetic, talented playmaker, he could give Spain the edge in Group A.

Dimitar Berbatov

Country | Bulgaria   **Position** | Striker   **Date of Birth** | 30.01.1981   **Club** | Bayer Leverkusen, Germany

A natural goalscorer who only needs one chance to find the back of the net. He relishes the biggest stage and has performed well in the Champions League, reaching the 2002 final against Real Madrid.

Ever since the 1994 World Cup when Bulgaria finished third, the nation has been looking for a new hero. Ten years later, Euro 2004 could be the start of a spectacular international career for Berbatov.

He will be the main supply of goals for a Bulgarian side that could surprise Italy, Sweden and Denmark in Group C. Just 23 years old, the pressure will be enormous but he is a tall, strong forward who should be able to handle himself.

In his five seasons with Bayer Leverkusen, Berbatov has already experienced a lot, and this summer's tournament in Portugal could be the greatest adventure yet.

Kevin Kuranyi

Country | Germany   **Position** | Striker   **Date of Birth** | 02.03.1982   **Club** | Stuttgart, Germany

Not many people expect Germany to play exciting football at Euro 2004, but with Kuranyi in their ranks they might not have any choice!

The tall marksman has been enjoying his time with high-flying Stuttgart. He's so good he's been linked with a potential move to Italy.

A transfer abroad would probably appeal to Kuranyi – after all, his family comes from all over the world. He was born in Brazil, and explains that he has, "Brazilian flair and German discipline." His mother is Panamanian, while his father was born in France and raised in Stuttgart. He also has a great-grandfather from Denmark, a grandfather from Hungary, and, vitally, a German grandmother.

German fans must be relieved this young heart-throb chose their nation. That Brazilian flair could be just what they need.

Fun football facts for Euro 2004

- **IN GROUP D THE CZECH REPUBLIC** will want revenge over Germany for beating them 2–1 in the final of Euro 96. Then again, as Czechoslovakia they beat West Germany on penalties in the 1976 final.

- **HOLLAND WANT REVENGE OVER THE CZECHS** for beating them in the qualifying group, and against Germany for the 2–1 defeat by West Germany in the 1974 World Cup Final. Poor old Latvia don't want revenge on anyone, because this is their first tournament.

- **AT EURO 2000 GERMANY FINISHED BOTTOM** of a group including England, Romania and Portugal.

- **THE CLUB SIDES WITH THE MOST** players playing at Euro 2000 were Juventus of Italy and Galatasaray of Turkey (11 each). They were followed in joint second place by Barcelona of Spain and Liverpool of England (10 each).

- **BOTH ITALY AND FRANCE REACHED THE** Euro 2000 final from the penalty spot. Italy's semi-final with Holland had to go to penalties, while Zinedine Zidane scored a Golden Goal penalty to see off Portugal.

- **YUGOSLAVIA WERE NOT ALLOWED TO PLAY** at Euro 1992 – despite qualifying – because of United Nations sanctions against the war-torn country. So Denmark took their place – and won the tournament!

- **THE MOST GOALS EVER SCORED BY** an individual player in a single European Championship was nine, by France's great Michel Platini in 1984. Beat that, Zidane!

- **THE TEAM THAT SCORED THE LEAST** goals while winning this tournament was Italy in 1968 – they managed just three goals.

- **THE BIGGEST WINS EVER IN THE** final stages came in 1984, when France beat Belgium and Denmark beat Yugoslavia, both 5–0.

- **IN 2000, FRANCE BECAME THE FIRST** country ever to hold the title of World and European Champions at the same time. They won the 1998 World Cup on home soil, then lifted the European Championship trophy two years later.

- **THE ROYAL MINT PRODUCED A SPECIAL** two-pound coin in 1996 to celebrate England hosting the tournament.

- **AT EURO 2000, PORTUGAL'S FERNANDO COUTO** won a special Fair Play award for stopping Portuguese fans from booing the German national anthem.

- **ENGLAND'S EURO 2000 SQUAD INCLUDED JUST** one player who played abroad (Steve McManaman). Only Italy and Spain's squads had no such players, while Denmark had the most foreign-based players – 19.

European Championship All-time Table (Not including qualifying matches)

		P	W	D	L	F	A	Pts	AvgPts
1.	Germany*	33	17	10	6	49	31	44	1.33
2.	Holland	25	15	6	4	45	23	36	1.44
3.	France	23	12	6	5	40	29	30	1.30
4.	Italy	24	10	9	5	26	17	29	1.21
5.	Soviet Union**	22	9	6	7	26	22	24	1.09
6.	Spain	25	7	8	10	26	32	22	0.88
7.	England	23	7	7	9	25	26	21	0.91
8.	Portugal	13	7	3	3	19	10	17	1.31
9.	Denmark	20	5	4	11	22	33	14	0.70
10.	Belgium	16	5	3	8	16	28	13	0.81
11.	Czechoslovakia+	10	4	4	2	16	12	12	1.20
12.	Yugoslavia++	16	4	4	8	23	32	12	0.75
13.	Hungary	9	3	2	4	12	13	8	0.89
14.	Czech Rep	9	3	2	4	10	11	8	0.89
15.	Sweden	7	2	2	3	8	9	6	0.86
16.	Romania	13	1	4	8	11	19	6	0.46
17.	Bulgaria	5	2	1	2	6	8	5	1.00
18.	Scotland	6	2	1	3	4	5	5	0.83
19.	Croatia	4	2	0	2	5	5	4	1.00
20.	Rep Ireland	3	1	1	1	2	2	3	1.00
21.	Norway	3	1	1	1	1	1	3	1.00
22.	Serbia & Mont.	4	1	1	2	8	13	3	0.75
23.	Turkey	7	1	1	5	3	9	3	0.43
24.	Slovenia	3	0	2	1	4	5	2	0.67
25.	Wales	2	0	1	1	1	3	1	0.50
26.	Greece	3	0	1	2	1	4	1	0.33
27.	Switzerland	3	0	1	2	1	4	1	0.33
28.	Russia	3	0	1	2	4	8	1	0.33

* Includes West Germany.
** This is the old name for Russia, which has since split into a number of new countries. Today's Russia is in 28th place.
+ Separate from Czech Republic.
++ This is the old Yugoslavia, which used to contain Croatia and Slovenia. In 1996 it split into a number of new countries and is now called Serbia and Montenegro – in 22nd place.

Euro Quiz

Answers on page 59!

1 **CELTIC'S STILIAN PETROV** is the captain of which nation?

2 **HOW MANY GAMES** will be played at Euro 2004 in total – not including qualifiers?

3 **HOW MANY OF THE 16 COUNTRIES'** flags do NOT contain the colour red?

4 **ITALY'S ALESSANDRO DEL PIERO AND FRANCESCO TOTTI** have each played for just one club. Which ones?

5 **WHAT IS THE FRENCH TEAM'S NICKNAME?**

6 **AT THE SAME TIME** David Beckham joined Real Madrid, which English player left the Spanish club?

7 **IN WHICH CITY** was the Euro 2000 final played?

8 **FOUR YEARS AGO,** David Trezeguet scored France's famous extra-time winner against Italy in the final. But which Arsenal player had earlier equalized for France?

9 **WHO WERE THE FIRST** ever European Championship winners?

10 **HOW MANY TEAMS** competed in the first ever European Championship final tournament – then called the 'Nations Cup'?

11 **NAME THE ITALIAN REFEREE** famed for his bald head and frightening stare.

12 **WHO WAS TOP** scorer at Euro 96?

13 **WHAT IS PORTUGAL'S** world-famous south coast holiday region called?

14 **WHICH TEAM** did Holland knock out in their qualifying play-off?

15 **WHICH OF THESE CAPITAL CITIES** is more southerly – Lisbon, Madrid, Rome, Istanbul?

16 **NAME PORTUGAL'S MOST FAMOUS** former player, who amazed Benfica fans in the 1960s.

17 **WHO IS ENGLAND'S** record goalscorer?

18 **WHICH ENGLAND STAR** famously cried on the pitch at the 1990 World Cup?

19 **WHEN DID ALAN SHEARER** play his last game for England?

20 **NOW FOR A SERIOUSLY DIFFICULT QUESTION.** What connects Ludovic Magnin of Switzerland with Albania's Ardian Aliaj? Need a clue? They should have carried a four leaf clover!

21 **WALES PULLED OFF ONE OF THE GREATEST RESULTS** in their history in October 2002 – who did they beat?

22 **WHAT ARE ENGLAND CAPTAIN** David Beckham's middle names?

23 **WHO BEAT ENGLAND** on penalties in the 1996 semi-final?

24 **SWEDEN'S 2003 FOOTBALLER OF THE YEAR** plays for Aston Villa. What's his name?

25 **THIERRY HENRY AND DAVID TREZEGUET** have BOTH played for which two clubs?

26 **TRUE OF FALSE:** this is the first time Greece have ever qualified for the European Championship.

27 **WHICH FOUR COUNTRIES** were unbeaten in the qualifying groups?

28 **WHAT IS THE CAPITAL** of Portugal?

29 **WHICH COACH SAID,** 'It was important to avoid Portugal and France'?

30 **A CZECH PAPER SAID** their national manager will have to perform magic like who...? Gandalf, Harry Potter, Monkey Boy or David Blaine?

Crossword

Answers on page 61!

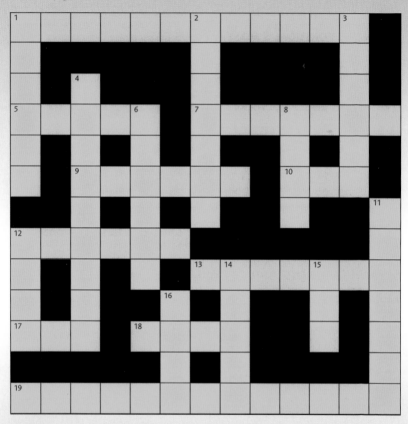

Across

1. England's talented captain (5, 7)
5. Sven-... Eriksson, the England Coach (5)
7. Chelsea midfielder, Frank... (7)
9. The French man they call Zizou (6)
10. Two yellows equals... (3)
12. Portuguese word for 'English' (6)
13. Freddie Ljungberg's club (7)
17. Goal! The ball's in the back of the... (3)
18. First name of Neville and Lineker (4)
19. Euro trophy is named after this Frenchman (5,8)

Down

1. Portugal stadium named after mythical beast (6)
2. Owen Hargreaves plays for which national side? (7)
3. Raul's favourite city? (6)
4. France hero, David... (9)
6. Czech Cannon – Pavel... (6)
8. Portugal's most famous type of wine (4)
11. Young Newcastle striker who won't be in Portugal (7)
12. Hero, legend or something on your computer screen (4)
14. Meaning of 'Real' in 'Real Madrid' (5)
15. Another word for zero, i.e. no goals (3)
16. Danish striker or type of castle (4)

Wordsearch

Answers on page 61!

N	Y	G	E	L	I	L	I	S	C	R	P	T	M	S	P	P	T	R	I
S	C	A	P	T	A	I	N	D	R	N	I	S	L	S	O	C	R	P	T
R	O	L	N	D	T	S	H	H	M	E	H	T	N	A	A	R	N	L	P
L	O	Y	Y	D	Z	B	H	R	F	B	S	O	K	Q	M	C	V	S	O
M	R	T	N	I	S	O	T	R	F	N	H	X	G	E	B	O	W	P	R
S	F	W	L	N	F	N	B	Y	O	S	A	H	E	R	O	E	S	O	T
S	A	T	H	M	P	N	D	I	N	R	T	M	C	H	V	R	G	D	U
P	N	L	K	N	F	R	P	W	D	T	M	I	T	E	E	M	W	N	G
A	S	I	D	T	Z	M	N	S	L	Y	U	M	M	A	T	T	A	F	A
I	T	T	H	N	A	H	T	V	C	N	F	U	S	S	C	D	C	H	L
F	U	N	A	H	E	X	S	E	S	H	S	V	I	F	S	M	S	E	R
G	R	J	C	D	M	K	L	N	S	K	O	L	R	K	Y	G	O	N	V
B	T	W	Y	Y	I	L	L	F	N	D	V	L	T	H	T	O	W	R	Z
L	S	A	F	R	N	U	C	H	A	E	N	D	E	I	D	G	E	Y	I
V	E	H	R	W	U	N	M	O	R	I	R	L	U	S	Y	F	N	C	Y
L	S	R	A	M	R	D	S	G	P	Y	T	H	R	H	V	N	G	O	P
T	T	Z	B	T	H	R	O	B	S	T	B	I	O	F	A	H	R	R	S
M	I	B	Y	R	D	A	X	Q	F	T	R	O	P	H	Y	T	H	Q	F
S	W	E	N	G	L	A	N	D	T	R	P	P	E	C	R	Z	Y	D	R
T	H	Q	S	B	C	R	P	T	S	B	T	T	I	O	N	K	I	Z	T

ANTHEM	LISBON
CAPTAIN	OWEN
CHAMPIONS	PORTUGAL
ENGLAND	SCHOLES
EUROPE	SILVER GOAL
FANS	STADIUM
HENRY	SVEN
HEROES	TROPHY

Fill-in Chart

Saturday June 12, 2004: The big kick-off on the big day. Hosts Portugal and a fired-up Greece will be ready to contest the very first match of the tournament. Portugal will be keen to show that they merit their automatic qualification...

The next four pages are not only your full guide to all the matches and kick-off times, but you can use them to follow your team's progress through the finals. Fill in the scores, tables and players for the final for your own personal record of the tournament. Will you be filling in an England team in the space for July 4?

Group A

1 Saturday June 12 – 5.00 p.m.
Portugal v Greece
Dragao, Porto

2 Saturday June 12 – 7.45 p.m.
Spain v Russia
Algarve, Faro/Loulé

9 Wednesday June 16 – 5.00 p.m.
Greece v Spain
Bessa, Porto

10 Wednesday June 16 – 7.45 p.m.
Russia v Portugal
Luz, Lisbon

17 Sunday June 20 – 7.45 p.m.
Russia v Greece
Algarve, Faro/Loulé

18 Sunday June 20 – 7.45 p.m.
Spain v Portugal
Jose Alvalade, Lisbon

Group B

3 Sunday June 13 – 5.00 p.m.
Switzerland v Croatia
Estadio Municipal de Leiria

4 Sunday June 13 – 7.45 p.m.
France v England
Luz, Lisbon

11 Thursday June 17 – 5.00 p.m.
England v Switzerland
Municipal, Coimbra

12 Thursday June 17 – 7.45 p.m.
Croatia v France
Estadio Municipal de Leiria

19 Monday June 21 – 7.45 p.m.
Croatia v England
Luz, Lisbon

20 Monday June 21 – 7.45 p.m.
Switzerland v France
Municipal, Coimbra

<table>
<tr><td colspan="2">

Group C

</td></tr>
</table>

Group C	Group D

Group C

5 Monday June 14 – 5.00 p.m.	D
Denmark v Italy	O
Afonso Henriques, Guimarães	

5	**6 Monday June 14 – 7.45 p.m.**
	Sweden v Bulgaria	O
	Jose Alvalade, Lisbon

13 Friday June 18 – 5.00 p.m.	
Bulgaria v Denmark	
Municipal, Braga	

14 Friday June 18 – 7.45 p.m.	
Italy v Sweden	
Dragao, Porto	

21 Tuesday June 22 – 7.45 p.m.	
Denmark v Sweden	
Bessa, Porto	

22 Tuesday June 22 – 7.45 p.m.	
Italy v Bulgaria	
Afonso Henriques, Guimarães	

Group D

1	**7 Tuesday June 15 – 7.45 p.m.**	1
	Germany v Holland
	Dragao, Porto

2	**8 Tuesday June 15 – 5.00 p.m.**	1
	Czech Republic v Latvia
	Municipal, Aveiro

15 Saturday June 19 – 5.00 p.m.	
Latvia v Germany	
Bessa, Porto	

16 Saturday June 19 – 7.45 p.m.	
Holland v Czech Republic	
Municipal, Aveiro	

23 Wednesday, June 23 – 7.45 p.m.	
Germany v Czech Republic	
Jose Alvalade, Lisbon	

24 Wednesday, June 23 – 7.45 p.m.	
Holland v Latvia	
Municipal, Braga	

Answers: Crossword and Wordsearch

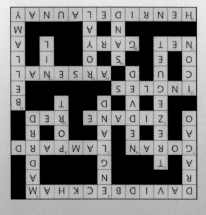

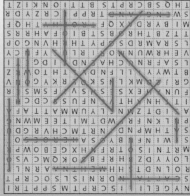

GROUP A – FINAL TABLE
Portugal; Greece; Spain; Russia

Team	P	W	D	L	F	A	Pts
1							
2							
3							
4							

GROUP B – FINAL TABLE
France; England; Switzerland; Croatia

Team	P	W	D	L	F	A	Pts
1							
2							
3							
4							

GROUP C – FINAL TABLE
Bulgaria; Denmark; Italy; Sweden

Team	P	W	D	L	F	A	Pts
1							
2							
3							
4							

GROUP D – FINAL TABLE
Latvia; Holland; Germany; Czech Republic

Team	P	W	D	L	F	A	Pts
1							
2							
3							
4							